Poems of Another Age

THE KEEPER AND HIS LAD

Cy McLatchie
the Keeper

and

Greg McLatchie
the Lad

OFFOX PRESS

British Library Catalogue in Publication Data
A catalogue record for this book is available in the British Library

ISBN 978-1-904202-02-8

Designed and set by Oxford Art and Design, Oxford
Printed and bound in Great Britain by Alden HenDi Ltd, Witney

ACKNOWLEDGEMENTS

I wish to thank Pamela Lines for her patient and diligent preparation
of the manuscript, and Colin Lines, Norrie MacLeod and June Mathieson for
the excellent photography. For support and advice I am indebted to Lynton Guest
and Doug Gillon, Louise Allison of Oxford Art and Design, and
Jackie Gray and John Churchill of Offox Press.
Greg McLatchie

Thornhill from Blacknest Farm.

Poems of Another Age

The Keeper and His Lad

CONTENTS

Foreword *(Doug Gillon)*	vi	Eddie *(1962)*	20
Introduction *(Lynton Guest)*	ix	Teachers *(1963)*	22
Preface *(Greg McLatchie)*	xiii	The Teacher's Reply *(1963)*	23
The Keeper *(1958)*	1	A Fancy from Fontenelle	23
Blacknest *(1958)*	2	Destiny *(1963)*	24
A Winter's Nicht *(1958)*	4	French Girls *(1963)*	26
Winter *(1959)*	6	Silly Willie *(1963)*	27
A Fisherman's Tale *(1959)*	8	Christine Keeler *(1963)*	30
The Poet *(1960)*	10	Pub Talk *(1964)*	32
Tess, a Farmer's Dog *(1961)*	12	Governor Wallace *(1964)*	33
To Mrs Syme's Cat, Frisky *(1961)*	14	The Reverend William Syme *(1964)*	34
The Passing of Sheila *(1961)*	15	Nithsdale *(1964)*	36
Around Blacknest Woods *(1962)*	16	Beauty *(1964)*	38
Youthful Delinquency *(1962)*	18	She Wasn't Really That Good-looking *(1964)*	39
Maidens *(1962)*	19		

Poems of Another Age

The Keeper and His Lad

CONTENTS

A Summary of Tonight *(1964)*	40
Politics *(1964)*	42
Drumlanrig *(1965)*	43
The Apology *(1965)*	44
Sussies on the Buses *(2008)*	45
Logging *(1973)*	46
On Winning *(1965)*	48
The Fly in the Inkwell *(1965)*	49
To a Critic *(1965)*	50
Kathleen *(1966)*	51
Kirkpatrick McMillan *(1966)*	52
There's Nothing That I Feel Now *(1966)*	54
The Present *(1966)*	55
Hogmanay *(1967)*	56
Travels *(1967)*	58
Brains Beat Bugs *(1967)*	59
Tim – No Ordinary Cat *(1967)*	60
The Fox Hunt *(1967)*	62
Morton Castle *(1967)*	64
My Future Has Been Changed *(1967)*	66
In Love Again *(1967)*	68
A Name is Not Beautiful *(1967)*	69
It Seems Strange *(1968)*	70
The Moon Laughed at Us *(1968)*	71
Absence Not Fonder Renders *(1968)*	72
How Will It Be? *(1968)*	74
My Sons *(1968)*	76
The House on the Moor *(1968)*	78
The Gamekeeper *(1968)*	80

FOREWORD

It was 1958, and a cold snap was forecast for the depths of Nithsdale. The Sunday school class in Thornhill was asked to write or draw something inspired by Jack Frost. Greg McLatchie, the eight-year-old son of the local gamekeeper, wrote a poem which was published in the kirk magazine.

This helped inspire a lifelong love of language and prompted his father, Cyril, who had previously shown no inclination for writing poetry, to write some of his own. For 10 years he helped young Greg with essays and poems, sometimes to the youngster's frustration 'because he was better than me.'

But there was more to it than just being a dad and helping with the homework. Even his English teacher remarked on the change of writing style when dad had helped, or had not.

Cyril wrote on the back of Christmas cards, or any handy scraps of paper when the muse struck him, but this creativity stopped abruptly when his son left for medical school: 'You're on your own now, son.' Father, then 63, wrote one last poem, 'The Gamekeeper'. It perceptively reflects the toughness of his life, but is also a commentary on the gulf between Britain's social classes.

That he should address this, and many other aspects of rural life, his family, and poaching, was hardly surprising. However, many topical subjects were remarkable for a man of his apparently artisan background – an excoriating critique of segregationist Alabama Governor George Wallace; a sympathetic and witty item on Christine Keeler and the events that helped discredit the Macmillan government, and bring it down in 1963; and another on the run-in to the 1964 general election when the Tories were led by Sir Alex Douglas-Home, who often shot on the estate where Cyril was employed.

Greg was two when his parents moved with his brother and sister into a semi-detached cottage, a tied house on the Duke of Buccleuch's estate south east of Thornhill. It had no modern toilet facility or electricity when they moved in. There were five acres on which the family could grow crops, graze livestock, rear pheasants and train dogs, and father could engage with the local gentry who clearly enjoyed his company.

They probably regarded this chess-playing, self-taught intellectual as something of an enigma. Indeed, as he marks the twenty-fifth anniversary of his father's death with this modest but fascinating wee anthology of his own and his father's writings, the son finds his father an enigmatic figure. Greg is unsure whether he is in search of his dad, but I believe he has already found him. In 2002, while continuing to work as a surgeon, he graduated with the law degree which his father was denied.

When father and son began writing poetry in 1958 they had no television. They listened as a family to the radio. The only newspapers to come into the house were the Sunday Post and News of the World. When his children showed signs of academic prowess, the Observer was purchased on Sundays.

This was a rapidly changing world. It was the year of the Munich air disaster which destroyed Matt Busby's 'Babes', of the first US satellite in space, Elvis joining the draft, Brazil's first World Cup win, the unveiling of the Bubble Car at the Motor Show, the inauguration of John Paul XXIII as Pope, and Charles de Gaulle as President of France, the opening of Britain's first eight miles of motorway, and the first parking meters in London.

By the time the elder McLatchie felt compelled to lash George Wallace ('I say segregation now, segregation tomorrow, segregation forever!'), TV had arrived in the household, and it allowed Cyril to broaden his range of commentary. He evolved into something of a philosopher, a man of high moral principle, and there is a perceptive item, a warning to his son on his departure for medical school, about people 'too greedy to be ill'.

Cyril McLatchie was born in 1906, the third eldest of 13 children. He won a scholarship to go to further education at 14. He wanted to study law, but like so many of his time the family could not afford University and so he became a metaphor for his generation. Leaving school at

14 he went to work as a gardener, then as a rabbit-trapper. He augmented his income as a boxer, fighting in booths, which was subsequently banned. He must have been a decent fighter for he survived with his marbles intact, and in 1930 he won £25 for one contest. A farm labourer then earned just under £6 for a 47-hour week.

But Cyril was not impoverished. He trapped rabbits by the thousand, and owned a 500cc motorbike which he raced on Solway Sands. Cyril was turned down for military service because of an arm injury, but it did not prevent him from being a crack shot. And rabbits, mentioned in song in 'Dad's Army' and an enormous nutritional resource, were a staple of the nation's wartime diet.

Given his father's boxing history, it is probably not entirely coincidental that while making his way in medicine, Greg McLatchie, with the pioneering neurosurgeon Bryan Jennett, co-authored a paper on head injury in sport. But his love of sport – various interests included being medical officer to the Martial Arts Commission – was seen as professionally inadvisable. He was warned by superiors that his sports medicine crusade was career threatening, that it was a pseudo-science, and to desist. Now a consultant surgeon at North Tees and Hartlepool NHS Trust, he became inaugural director of the National Sports Medicine Institute in 1992, and is Professor of Sports Medicine at the University of Sunderland, the first chair of sports medicine in the UK.

'I just threw a few pebbles in a pond, and the ripples hit every shore,' said Greg. 'Within 18 months, there were seven chairs of sports medicine at British universities.'

Though his father abandoned writing at the age of 63, Greg McLatchie continues to write poetry. That's why he has decided to mark the 25th anniversary of his father's death with this book.

Doug Gillon,
Glasgow

INTRODUCTION

I met Greg McLatchie in the early 1990s when he was the first Director of the National Sports Medicine Institute in London and I was a sports writer for the Sunday Telegraph. At that time he was working tirelessly to promote the cause of Sports Medicine to a then reluctant establishment. It is mainly due to Greg's efforts that the discipline is now a recognised medical speciality instead of merely being an adjunct to the study of soft tissue injuries in general, which was a reflection of its lowly status then. Today Sport and Exercise Medicine and its related discipline, Sports Science, is firmly situated at the glamour end of the medical spectrum. It attracts large numbers of students and not a little research cash. Having withdrawn from the NSMI once the groundwork was complete, Greg himself has never profited from the resulting success.

Since we hit it off so well, I often visited Greg at his home in Hartlepool. There he was, and remains, a surgeon at the University Hospital and a Professor at the University of Sunderland. He not only combined this work with his stint at the NSMI, but also wrote two classic text books for aspiring surgeons published by Oxford University Press, and lately also by Harvard University Press in the United States.

If this were not enough, I have another story. Greg was club doctor for a professional rugby club, West Hartlepool, and one day invited me to sit on the bench with him during a crunch encounter for promotion to the Premier League against Saracens. All went well for seventy-odd minutes, allowing me to really enjoy my privileged position (Hartlepool won a great game but just missed out on promotion that year). Then, one

of West's players lost what looked like most of his ear, Evander Holyfield style, in a melee not five yards from where I was sitting. Whilst I was quietly but desperately turning away from the bloody mess before me, Greg, the consummate professional, took him to the medical room from where he returned stitched and bandaged, to resume play. All this was done without fuss and the player completed the game.

Apart from all these activities, I suppose what really endeared me to Greg was the fact that, as such a fine surgeon, he could have commanded an indecent amount of money had he chosen to ply his capabilities in the private sector. However, he has always remained committed to the National Health Service and I believe that this is really to be applauded.

One day something remarkable occurred. After a few beers in a local hostelry, Greg began to talk about his father. This man was immense. He had been a boxer in fairground booths between the wars when such an occupation could easily get a man killed. Later he became a gamekeeper on the estate of the Duke of Buccleuch in southern Scotland, but he also wrote poems, and Greg showed me some of them. I thought then, and believe still, that the qualities these poems display are of the highest order. Moreover, inspired by his father's example, Greg confessed to being a closet poet. I knew he liked poetry – after all he hails from Burns Country – but I never realised that he could write the stuff himself.

The examples in this volume were written by Cy or Greg in the main between 1958 and 1968. I remember those years particularly for the Beatles, steam trains, and a yearning to live where all the action was supposed to happen – London. Although from different parts of the land, Greg and I recognise something we have in common from our upbringings during that tumultuous period. From post-war austerity our generation went on to change the world, although anyone over 30 was considered extremely suspect. We did acknowledge the importance of many of those who went before – Aldous Huxley, for instance, especially his great work the 'The Doors of Perception' (from which Jim Morrison took the name 'The Doors'), which was a particular icon, but reading Greg's dad's verse I realised that awareness and radical thought existed throughout the country, indeed throughout the world and, more importantly, across generational boundaries. It was a beautiful moment.

The poems in this book show us that radical ideas cascade through time and we owe a debt to those who came before us. Greg's response mirrors the world we were about to unleash. Of all included here, my favourite is the poem about George Wallace confronting the pernicious and destructive issue of racism yet managing to do so ironically and with great beauty in the pay-off line. This is the stuff which can challenge our preconceptions and make us open our minds. I suggest you read these works again and again, enjoy them, love them.

Lynton Guest,
Egham

The hills above Durisdeer

The Nith Valley from Glenim

PREFACE

Mid-Nithsdale begins at Glenairlie and ends at Auldgirth. The area, about 11 miles long and equally broad, forms a valley almost completely encircled by hills, the only openings being where the river Nith enters and leaves this basin. To the east are the Closeburn and Morton Hills which unite with the green, billowy Lowthers in the north. On the west side the gentle Keir range joins with the Tynron and Penport Hills to form a beautifully picturesque but irregular barrier to the outside world. Cairnkinna (1,819 feet) lies northwest and Queensberry (2,285 feet) in the east make up this great natural rampart.

In the virtual centre of this valley lies the village of Thornhill, the capital of Mid-Nithsdale. Its modern, wide streets are lined with beautiful lime trees and, more recently, boutique shops. The streets run north to south and east to west. At their confluence stands the Village Cross, octagonal in form, with its spaces divided into neat panels. From its centre rises a fluted Corinthian column surmounted by a bronze Pegasus, the wingèd horse which sprang from the blood of Medusa. With a blow of his hoof he caused the fountain of the Muses to spring from Mount Helicon. Bellerophon mounted him and with his aid destroyed the Chimaera. This statue was erected by the Duke of Queensberry in 1714. It is a feature of daily life and Fairs, ancient and now modern, are traditionally held around it.

East Morton Street, or The Gill as it is called locally, leads to the school, cemetery, golf course and to Laught Blacknest, two semi-detached cottages about one and a half miles south-east of the village. It was to here that my father came, in 1952, on becoming a gamekeeper to the Duke of Buccleuch. Formerly he had been a rabbit-trapper, but myxomatosis and post-war relaxation on rationing put an end to that occupation.

I was two years old. The cottage – two up, two down – had no modern toilet or electricity but these were added as part of the employment contract. The house was rent free for as long as my father was employed by the Duke, and an adjacent five acre field (named Cowgang) was included.

Cy feeding guinea fowl and ducks on our smallholding

My father used the field to grow crops, graze cows and sheep, and rear pheasants in successive years. Our smallholding was vibrant with pigs, ducks, sheep and cattle. He kept and trained around seventeen dogs for various owners and the house was always busy. The local doctor, lawyer, and minister were regular visitors. They kept dogs or went shooting there, and my father loved nothing better than holding court with them about catching vermin, fishing, snaring foxes or the price of pelts.

Cyril was also a lay lawyer and assisted many locals with legal matters. My mother Jean, a canny lady, kept a beautifully clean house and turned us all out immaculately for school. She was also a wonderful cook. Neilson, my brother, left home to do national service when I was three. I and my sister Kathleen, who was two years older than me, were brought up in what I now realise were very privileged circumstances.

My father was always interested in poetry but had never written any until in 1958, when I presented my first attempt at writing poetry, 'A Winter's Nicht', to the local minister. For the next ten years my father regularly wrote poems and essays (usually with me). When I went to University in 1968, he promptly stopped!

This year (2008) marks the twenty-fifth anniversary of Cyril McLatchie's death, and I look back on the enigma that was my father with curiosity and pride. His was a hard life and he was a hard man. He was also an independent intellectual who ploughed his own furrow and ensured that I had the education which he would have wished for himself.

Greg McLatchie,
Hartlepool

1958

THE KEEPER

This was a popular song in the 1950s and 1960s which my father often used to sing.
I don't know who the author was.

When the auld cock crows
Everybody knows
Ye're sure tae see the keeper in the morning.

Well, I know all the habits
Of the simple-minded rabbits
Sometimes I'm fast enough tae catch a hare.
And ye may take my word
I'm as fond of every bird
.... But since I'm a married man
I'll say nae mair!

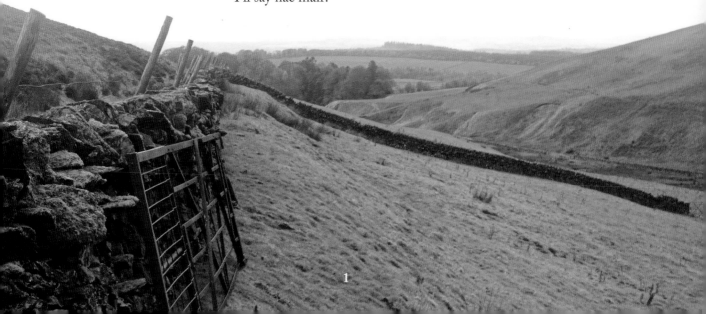

BLACKNEST

Gregor McLatchie is my name.
Scotland is my nation.
Blacknest is my dwelling place –
My place of habitation.

When I'm dead and in my grave
And all my bones are rotten
This little book will tell you all
That I am not forgotten!

G.McL. & C.McL.

Gregor McLatchie

Blacknest in autumn

A WINTER'S NICHT

*This was a competition run by the Sunday school. The Reverend William Syme
warned us of the impending cold snap that was due to hit the village and its surroundings,
and asked us to write, draw or create something about Jack Frost. This was my effort.
Miss Mary Shuttleworth, our Sunday school teacher, thought it was good
and it was published in the Church magazine.*

A Winter's nicht is very dreary
And mak's ye think that Jackie's near ye
It's him wha clim's upon the wa'
And sends us nocht but sleet an' snawe
And mak's us chitter[1] mair an' mair
'Til teeth and banes start tae get sair
Sae, mothers, keep yer bairnies warm
In Winter's cauld and weary storm!

G.McL.

[1]*chitter – shiver*

A Winter's nicht ...

WINTER

Mrs Houston was an unusual teacher.
Although she addressed the curriculum, she encouraged her pupils
to be creative. Snow began to fall one day in December 1959 and she
suspended classes and asked the pupils to describe or draw what
they saw and felt.

Snow was falling on the ground
And whirling flakes went round and round.
Icicles hanging from the trees
Sparked brightly in the breeze
. . . And all was quiet around and cold!

Cold nips my fingers and my toes
Although I wear my thickest clothes
A pain's now ringing in my ears
And in my eyes a tear appears
As I hurry home at e'en.

The robin on the window-sill
Shivers in the Winter's chill
And hopes a few crumbs I will give
That through these cold days he may live
And sing his song in Spring.

But, now a sweet thought fills my heart.
I know that this is just the part
Between the Autumn and the Spring.
Spring, that time so fascinating
When all the little birds are mating
And sing their songs to me.

I know that I will have the heart
Throughout my life to do my part
And even in the darkest night
Will only do what I think right
And always be the man!

G.McL. & C.McL.

Greg with his son Calum and their friend Leanne

A FISHERMAN'S TALE

This poem relates to my first attempt at fishing. Bob Kerr, the greenkeeper at Thornhill golf course, used bamboo rods to sweep worm casts off the greens. I asked if they would make good fishing rods so he gave me one, some string, and a loop of gut with hooks and a sinker. My sister Kate and I set off for Cample, a stream about a mile away. I returned an hour or so later with a 1lb brown trout!

A lad o' nine went oot tae fish one cloudy summer's night.
Wi' keen young eye he scanned the sky
And thocht his prospects bright
He'd howkit worms his tin tae fill
Aye thinkin' o' the fish he'd kill
And when, at length, of worms he'd ample
He toddled down the road to Cample.

He'd heard o' thae great fishin' tales
O' fish full three feet lang.
And in his joy, this fisher boy, began tae sing a sang.
The fish that he wad catch the day
Would surely be a sample
O' the biggest fish that e'er was pu'd
Oot o' a' the Cample.

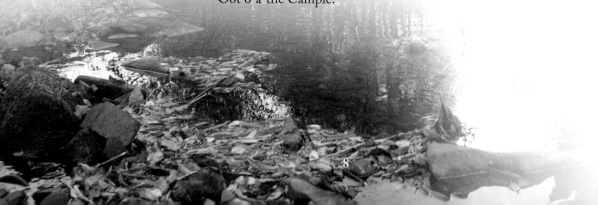

He sat him doon tae contemplate
On where his line he'd shoot
Then warily keekit up and doon
Tae see if the keeper wis aboot.
Wi' hazel rung[1] and bended preen[2]
It wis his dearest wish
That he'd hae peace for half an 'oor
Tae let him catch his fish

Wi' serious face he cast his line
Into the gurgling waters.
(There wasnae time tae concentrate
On other silly matters)
Then, joy of joys, he felt a tug
His patience was rewarded
When lying on the gravel there
His fish he now regarded.

He thought of when he went to school
The lads would round him meet
Tae listen to his story
Of this, his greatest feat
He'd ne'er let on it wis sae wee
There's nae doot it wis bonnie
As Rabbie[3] said, 'Aye keep something tae yersel
Ye scarcely tell tae ony!'[4]

C.McL.

[1]*hazel rung – wooden rod*

[2]*bended preen – bent pin*

[3]*Rabbie – Robert Burns*

[4]*'Aye…tae ony' – always keep something to
yourself you'd rarely tell to anyone else!*

Cample Water

THE POET

Peer pressure and rivalry were the norm at Morton Academy. If you liked language you just did not fit in and some of the penalties were cruel. This retort was in response to a bullying episode I experienced. The boys just wanted me to play football, not write words. I suppose the modern day equivalent is to be a team player. Pioneers are passé.

I'm asked to prove that I'm a poet
And by my powers I'll try to do it
I must admit it's kind of hard
Tae prove mysel' a worthy bard
. . . . at sic short notice.

But if you'll only gie me time
Tae spin a verse or twa o' rhyme
I'll send it tae ye at yer hame
Where ye can read it a' yer lane
. . . . if only for a laugh!

G.McL.

The poet (Greg) in the old car

TESS, A FARMER'S DOG

Robert Mair (Bob) was the farmer at Blacknest farm. We collected our daily milk from there, a return walk of about one mile. He had a border collie called Tess who was run over but survived.

Auld Tess, when she is in the light
Her body shows up broon and white.
She's clever, tough an' petted tae
An' rounds Bob's sheep up every day.
Every morning just at eight
She drives the coos up through the gate
She's very faithful to her master
And never fails to do what he asks her.

One day when Tess went on the rake
A driver who was slow to brake
Hit the puir creature sic a crack,
The wallop nearly broke her back.
She crawled into the hedge so thick
An' there her wounds began tae lick
An' tho' she felt sae awfy lame
She struggled up and made for hame.

Bob nursed puir Tess for full six weeks
An' wrapped her up in his auld breeks
Tae keep her clear o' ony chill
For he kent Tess wis feelin' ill.
But now she is as right as rain
And roundin' up Bob's sheep again.

G.McL.

'Her body shows up broon and white.'

Ploughing at Blacknest Farm

13

TO MRS SYME'S CAT, FRISKY

*Mrs Syme was the minister's wife, and I didn't like her. My mother used
to clean her house. I didn't know the word then but she was patronising. Note the contrast
in language between this poem and that written to her husband,
the Reverend William Syme, BSc (page 34).*

Dear Mrs Syme, I could have cried,
When Mummy told me your cat had died
May God be with you in your sorrow
And bring you a new joy tomorrow.
May you find some thoughts of gladness
Even in this hour of sadness
In the thought that now she'll rest
With the cats that love of God has blest!

G.McL.

THE PASSING OF SHEILA

*Sam Maxwell was the gamekeeper at Cample, now
a riding school. He kept terriers. This relates to the response, or apparent
response, of the survivor of two dogs after one died overnight.*

The home by Cample, once happy and gay
Is now draped in sorrow – poor Sheila's away
And even the morning can bring no relief
To poor little Don who is stricken with grief
Through all the long night his love never veered
But he stood o'er her 'til her master appeared
The love of this dog like the bright summer sky
Is a sweet thing of beauty, no money can buy!

C.McL.

View from Blacknest over the golf course towards Thornhill

AROUND BLACKNEST WOODS

A lot of time in my childhood was spent with animals. There was no television, only radio, and the lads in the village lived one and half miles away. So bonds were formed. Tim was my cat and I thought he was rather special. He was killed by a car and had been missing for three days before I found him in a wood where he had been thrown.

Around Blacknest woods, when Timmy was nigh
No poor Scottish boy was as happy as I
But now that he's left me . . . oh lonely the day
No more will we frolic o'er the golf course at play.
Black was his body and white was his chest
And of all of our cats I thought him the best
But now that he's dead his hunger will cease
For in the Cats' Heaven he now rests in peace.

G.McL.

Blacknest Woods

Thornhill Clubhouse

YOUTHFUL DELINQUENCY

A young lad of twelve threw a rubber eraser in a bus.
It bounced around hitting people. He was reported to the police and had
to appear before the local magistrate.

When I was but a boy of twelve I was a playful lad
In fact, many of our neighbours even thought me bad.
But when I threw a rubber in the local bus
Of this wicked deed of mine there really was a fuss.
I was summonsed to appear before the local magistrate
Who with a serious countenance did all my sins relate.
My villainy was the worst he'd ever heard about
In other words he made it clear that I was just a lout!
Who was this man who spoke such words about the deed I'd done?
For to my mind it was nothing more than just a bit of fun.
I saw a face with paunchy eyes caused by dissipation
And the smell which emanated was of a Scotch creation!
I wondered how a man like this could sit with serious face
And tell me how this act of mine had left me in disgrace.
I've met many men like this, who pretend they do no evil
Yet, often in their private lives, their acts would shame the devil!

C.McL.

MAIDENS

In 1962 we had our first television delivered. Dad loved it. This was his response to a news item relating to new fashions in women's clothes.

Young maidens all in days of yore
Were so demure and shy
Their dress of ankle length and more
Hid all from passers-by
Yet they had points of sex appeal
Their gorgeous flowing tresses
Now maids more subtle points reveal
Arrayed in topless dresses
See yon young rascal's roving eye
As he a maid is greeting
Then catch an eyeful on the sly
As he watches her retreating
She heeds not what his look implies
But merely winks and giggles
And just for provocation tries
To add those extra wiggles!

C.McL.

EDDIE

*This poem was written in response
to the reaction of my sister and myself to
the death of our uncle Edward, who was my
mother's brother. He had been chief electrical
engineer on board a merchantman of the Blue
Funnel Line, and in retirement ran an electrical
business on the White Sands in Dumfries. In the
1950s he had been responsible for the electrical
fitments in many buildings in Dumfries,
including the Cairndale Hotel.*

*Uncle Eddie was generous, and regaled us
with stories of the sea, and what we now know
to be 'Tsunamis'.*

Through coming years will I remember
That day of sorrow in September.
The nurse, by phone, had made us ready
To hear sad news of Uncle Eddie.
We walked around the room in tears
Thinking of the happy years
That we had spent together.
Could Cruel Fate part us forever?
What could our leaden hearts beguile
When never more we'd see his smile?

We stood around our loved one's grave
And bowed our heads in sorrow.
We thought of all the joys he gave
How could we face the morrow?
His humble countenance belied
The greatness of his mind.
This man who spent his life on earth
Loving human kind.
His memory leaves a wealth with us
No human hand can measure
For better far than gold or fame
Is this everlasting treasure!

C.McL.

Edward Grant on board M.V. Peisander

TEACHERS

Mr Patrick Walker was our geography teacher. He was the cousin of Patrick Gordon Walker MP, who was in the Wilson cabinet, and he took us for R.E. (religious education). On one occasion, he belted me for 'talking and distracting the class', in this instance wrongly, although I was usually guilty. I gave him this poem the following day.

The boxer vents his wrath
On his opponent in the ring
The wasp inflicts its enemy
With the venom of its sting.
But Mr Walker's subtle
In his method of attack
He wallops the poor pupil
Who cannot hit him back!
Why not exercise more patience
If in class we don't all fit?
For the dullest one amongst us
Is still a part of it.
Some people act mysteriously
For this accept my word
But when the pen's used as a defence
It's mightier than your sword.

G.McL.

Four or five days later, during geography class with Miss Brass, Mr Walker came in and quietly asked to speak to McLatchie. He then announced to the class that I was going to be taught a lesson for insubordination and disrespect of authority. He frogmarched me to the Rector's office, slammed the door, smiled and stretched out his hand saying, 'In the Wild West it would be guns at dawn!' for he knew I was interested in the American West. We shook hands, and he gave me his reply:

THE TEACHER'S REPLY

Dear Gregor, your apology is worth an answer yet,
For any idle pupil needs all that he should get
A wallop is forgotten after many happy days
But the misery of failure needs more than money pays.
No stupid, dull, unhappy ever felt this hand of mine
But, for the gifted and the lazy to waste God's gift is a crime.
And, Gregor, do not tell me that the last two lines don't rhyme,
For the assonance is perfect and it works eight times out of nine.

P. Walker

Some days later Mr Walker stopped me in the corridor and gave me a book of English verses, one of which he loved. It was entitled 'A Fancy from Fontenelle'.

A FANCY FROM FONTENELLE

'De mémoires de Roses on n'a point vu mourir le Jardinier'

The Rose in the garden slipped her bud,
And she laughed in the pride of her youthful blood,
As she thought of the Gardener standing by –
'He is old - so old! And he soon must die!'

The full Rose waxed in the warm June air,
And she spread and spread 'til her heart lay bare,
And she laughed once more as she heard his tread –
'He is older now! He will soon be dead!'

But the breeze of the morning blew, and found
That the leaves of the blown Rose strewed the ground;
And he came at noon, that Gardener old,
And he raked them gently under the mould.

And I wove the thing to a random rhyme,
'For the Rose is Beauty, the Gardener, Time.'

Austin Dobson

DESTINY

My father often observed that many people were more interested in making money than looking after themselves. When I started Medical School he told me that I'd see people who were 'too greedy to be ill'.

One evening in the month of June just shortly after ten
I wandered forth to meditate upon the ways of Men
To gain their ends they'll lose their friends
And even risk their health
In their eternal struggle – accumulating wealth.
There are those in sacred cloth who tell us of the need
To give up all material thoughts which stimulate our greed.
And yet, somehow, I've still to meet a man of destiny
Who'd willingly give up his gold for his eternity.
They speak of God as one to fear,
A spirit from above
But I accept him to revere
With everlasting love.
Men have gone this way through life,
Right from the start of time
And spoken of the pitfalls all along the line.
The man who loves his fellow-man,
'Tis he who stands the test
And when he comes to journey's end
His memory will be blessed.
Some men spend their time in pious meditation

Dalveen Pass

But thousands waste their youth in thoughtless dissipation
The vilest man is surely he who sins then blames another
When by all our human laws he should have called him brother.
In our walk through life let this be our plan
Never bear false witness against our fellow man
And so let one and all, all thoughts of falsehood dread,
And when we reach our end in life we go with upright head.

C.McL.

FRENCH GIRLS

French was a great experience and was emphasised by the arrival of a French Mademoiselle.
This was not, however, universally popular.

Some o' the louts at Morton school
Are trying hard tae mak' a fool
O' oor French teacher.
May their silly jibes ne'er reach her
For all these clowns wha look sae daft
May find French lassies no sae saft
She'll maybe teach these silly boys
That empty barrels mak' maist noise.

For myself', I think she's smart
And nae doot she will dae her part
Tae teach us a' at fools' expense
How vile and empty is their nonsense.

G.McL.

Morton School

SILLY WILLIE

William Mitchell was a greengrocer in Thornhill and he and my father were stalwart friends. Mr Mitchell had an easy and welcoming manner and often appeared surprised at what people divulged to him. My father kept his guns at Blacknest and on one occasion they had a hilarious evening talking about a recent episode when the police had detained some poachers and confiscated their guns and equipment. Dad and Mr Mitchell thought up the following ruse and Dad presented it to him in rhyme a few days later. Mr Mitchell was very astute. He 'keeked through every other man with sharpened sly inspection'. His statement: 'You only have one chance to make a first impression' has stuck in my memory and has been a very useful guide when interviewing or examining.

Folk ca' me Silly Willie and I come frae Thornhill
O' tricks played by the village boys, I've fairly had my fill.
There's some whose jokes are harmless, an' just done for a laugh
But others wi' their dirty tricks fairly blaw the gaff.[1]
There's some play tricks at school and then the teacher rants
He tak's his cane and fairly warms the hide below their pants.
Some mak their jokes wi' Hunt i' Gowk[2] and some wi' ba's o' snawe[3]
But the trick that Silly Willie played surely beats them a'.

It started yin cauld winter's day, ma bluid wis runnin' thin
And I wis wanderin' through the woods to see what I could fin'
When trailin' through some brammels a thorn got in ma foot.
To rid masel' o' this bad frien' I sat doon on a root
I had just ta'en off my boot and was feelin' o'er my sock
When in below a briar bus'[4] I spied a pheasant cock.
Now, how on earth could I resist this terrible temptation
That strong emotion all men feel in every kind of station.
I quickly took my hazel stick and hit it ower the heid
An' before I'd time tae draw a breath, the pheasant cock was deid.

Then when I saw what I had done an excited lad was I
But keekin' through a holly tree a wuman's face I spy
It wis Mully Gass frae New Street. She wis an awfu' blether
An' trouble she wad hae me in, if her tongue I couldna tether.
I quickly grabbed my pheasant cock and held my heid for hame.
Before ony other body could fin' oot my wee game
When I got home I wracked my brain tae think aboot a scheme
Tae make the keeper and polis think they'd had an awfu' dream.

I got masel' a lump o' clay and modelled it right weel
Then stuck tail feathers in the rump an' nae doot it looked real
I gathered up my masterpiece and put it in my bag
Then waited for the mornin' and the time began tae drag.
When mornin' came I donned my bag tail feathers stickin' oot
Then went tae hunt the keeper. I was sure he'd be aboot.
I very soon discovered Mully had done her job
I kent the silly body could nae haud her gob.
The keeper an' the bobbie were stannin' doon the hill
And judging by their gestures were bletherin' their fill.

I made my way oot through the wood and climbed oot owre the gate
And soon it was apparent the twa had ta'en the bait.
For baith o' them made after me as fast as they could go
But in my turn I made my way, my step was ought but slow
And when I got intae the toon I went wi' leaden feet
Just so that they'd catch up wi' me upon the busy street.
Which is just where they grabbed me an' each an airm did pin
And said to me, 'Come quietly, Wullie, we're gaun tae tak' ye in.'
Now, in atween these giants I looked sae awfy frail
As doon the street they marched me into the local jail
Now, in a place like Thornhill this caused a great commotion

And just confirmed in people's minds what once was just a notion
That Wullie was a poacher of the gravest order
Wha' ever killed a pheasant cock this side o' the border.
When in the jail they had me they coupit oot my bag
And keekin' up quite shyly I saw their faces sag.
For there before their starin' een my pheasant cock broke up
T'was then that they discovered I'd sold them baith a pup.[5]

Now wha' this simple tale may read may think that I'm a sinner
But I went boldly stridin' hame tae hae pheasant cock for dinner!

C.McL.

[1]blaw the gaff - went beyond reasonable limits
[2]Hunt i' Gowk - April Fool
[3]wi' ba's o' snawe - with snow balls
[4]a briar bus' - a thorny bush
[5]sold them baith a pup - tricked them

Thornhill

CHRISTINE KEELER

The Profumo affair rocked the Macmillan Government and led to its collapse. The Wilson Government (Labour) was voted into office. I am grateful for two things: I did not have to go to Vietnam and the Open University gave opportunities for massive educational change.

Sex is a favourite topic where men are congregated
Start a spicy story, they'll sit with breath abated.
Now, don't at my attitude, start complaining
Or pretend your sensual instinct's waning.
And I'll tell you of the sexy scenes
Of one of Piccadilly's Queens
For, as a saucy sex appealer
Few could beat young Christine Keeler.

She looks so fragile, this London maid
So ashen is her cheek.
She goes to church on Sunday with demeanour mild and meek.
A famous Russian diplomat loved to see her face
Resplendent of devotion, of purity and grace
And as he walked her home when services were o'er
He'd speak to her of Jesus and of the Golden Shore.
Young Christine shyly bowed her head, 'Oh Ivan dear' said she
'Nought in this world I would not give, the Golden Shore to see.'

This filled his being with desire
And set his sensual mind on fire
What joy 't would be, his thoughts ran wild,
To seduce this simple peasant child.
We'll to my luxury flat repair
And there we shall ourselves prepare.
Do as I do. Find nought amiss
And we'll attain that heavenly bliss.

What thoughts were in her mind is anybody's guess
As she watched dear Ivan shyly, whilst he helped her to undress
'Oh, my darling Ivan,' was all that maiden said
As he embraced her naked body and laid her on the bed.

When morning came the man arose, despondent and afraid
His conscience pricked him sorely and this to her he said,
'My darling child, I've ruined you, whatever shall I do?
I've stolen your virginity and lost my honour too.
My gracious Master, Kruschev, how will he bear the shame?
What terrible calamity I've brought upon my name!'

The maid looked up contemptuously and said with mock serenity,
'Don't worry, Ivan dear, o'er the loss of my virginity,
This will not boost your ego nor fill your heart with glee
I've shared with you the raunchy jaunt that playful Jack gave me

So if this gives you heartache
This to your Kruschev tell
You took a maid to heaven
But she sent you to Hell!'

C.McL.

PUB TALK

My father was a sociable man but he rarely drank alcohol. Only in his retirement did he buy and enjoy a bottle of whisky a week. This relates to a visit to the Buccleuch Hotel in Thornhill after a day's shooting in 1964.

I went into the local pub tae hae a pint o' beer,
The popular beverage men declare will bring about good cheer.
And as I stood beside the bar listening tae the patter
I decided tales like these were never brewed in water.
A gairdner bragged o'er frothy glass how well his roses bloomed
And better still his plants became the mair that he consumed.
Some 'herds were gathered in a bunch each at a whisky sippin'
Nae doot, by the way they spoke, they were a' adept at clippin'
A plooman staunin' at the bar had at his feet a cur[1]
He was tellin' folk aroon he could draw the straightest fur
Now, maybe he was tellin' lees or maybe speakin' true
But there's ae thing I'm certain o', he couldna dae it the noo!
Yin talked about the bonny pigs nursed by his large white soo
Anither a' aboot the milk ta'en frae his Ayrshire coo
While, further back a keeper lad sitting on a chair
Mentioned a' the clever ways that he could set a snare.
So, in conclusion, let me say, if aught should cause you trouble.
It maybe hoo tae big a dyke[2] or hoo tae ploo a stubble[3]
Or maybe tips on makin' grub, or cookin' Irish stew
Don't let your troubles get you down, there's really nothing new
Or if you're bothered socially, because you're no a dancer
Just take your worries tae the pub and there you'll find the answer.

G.McL. & C.McL.

[1]*Cur - dog*
[2]*Big a dyke - build a wall*
[3]*Ploo a stubble - plough a field*

GOVERNOR WALLACE

George Wallace was Governor of Alabama. He was, to say the least, controversial. This relates to an episode in which black children were killed in a church: 'The greatest wrong may still be right, if it's committed by a White!'

Blow the trumpets, beat the drums
Wave your banners, the hero comes
Serve succulent food, choice vintage wine
For this hero of Anglo-Saxon line
Let the gallant on the rostrum stand
Hark the music of the band
His stature's grown beyond his dreams
With those dying children's screams
They're celebrating Wallace day
In Alabama, USA.

Lest it be thought that I'm insane
I'll continue in more serious vein
This fiend, no doubt the vilest brute
That e'er the Devil did recruit
His just dessert would thus entail
A spike driven underneath each nail
Then when for mercy screams the lout
Shove another up his snout
And hope that we shall never find
His like again 'mongst human kind.

The story's end I'll now unfold
They've caught this Wallace, henchman bold
Who did, while in the shadows lurch
Throw the bomb into the church
Which tore those children limb from limb
Now will they justly punish him?
No, one hundred pounds they've fixed his bail
To buy his freedom from the jail
The cruellest deed may still be right
If it's committed by a White!

A coloured Preacher caused consternation
By attending to his congregation.
His crime, whilst visiting his charge?
He had no permit to be at large.
Nine hundred pounds they want, at least
To free this wicked, coloured priest.
Black is the future of a nation
Which permits such cruel discrimination
God, in your judgement punish them
Who shock all decent living men!

C.McL.

THE REVEREND WILLIAM SYME

Here was a really good man. Reverend Syme had been a pharmacist before becoming a minister and I really liked him. He took personal interest in the youngsters and used to hold Sunday School parties in the Manse. When I was leaving Morton Academy for Dumfries Academy he invited me and my father 'to fill the van' with as many books as we could. I still have most of them today, the oldest dating back to 1868 by Allan Ramsay, the Ettrick shepherd, and Robert Ferguson – both poets who predated and influenced Burns. Hence the Fergusonian (later Burnsian) stanzas.

The Manse is now owned by my friend Robert Mitchell, 'Silly Willie's' son!

And so it seems that once again
I lift my weary, wabbit[1] pen
An' only for tae let ye ken
A word or two,
It is with heartfelt joy I sen'
My thanks to you.

The books ye've gaen[2] ha'e filled oor van,
I never kenned my master plan.
But ye were canny[3] tae me scan
And rede[4] me weel
An' I think ye're baith a clever man
And decent chiel[5]!

G.McL.

[1]wabbit – tired
[2]gaen – given
[3]canny – careful
[4]rede – advise
[5]chiel – fellow

34

Morton Church

NITHSDALE

This is descriptive of the breathtaking natural beauty of the Nith valley, and also of the areas where my father worked.

Let other men boast of their cities so gay
Their clubs and their halls where famous stars play.
Not a fig do I care for their airs and their graces
I've lost my heart to the wide open spaces!

Down the Nith valley is a view I hold dear,
As I stand on the hillside above Durisdeer.
To the south lies the Solway, so quiet and so still
As I climb o'er the heights of bold Castlehill.

More Fairyland beauty to the north can be seen
The shepherd's lone homestead of Upper Dalveen,
And northward still further across Enterkin
Behold the wild beauty of the hills of Glenim.

What lovelier than Mennock can Nature display?
Where the hardy hill sheep so leisurely stray.
Far from the City so glaring and loud,
Far from its hurrying feverish crowd.
The heather-clad hillsides by Man not defiled.
My heart fills with awe at this beauty so wild.
There's music in the muircock's call
And gurgling of the waterfall.
From deep in my soul comes the urge to protect
This wondrous creation of the supreme architect.

C.McL.

at lovelier than Mennock can Nature display?

The Nith Bridge at Thornhill

Where the hardy hill sheep so leisurely stray . . .

37

To the South lies the Solway . . .

BEAUTY

Men have worshipped beauty right down through the ages.
Their words of adulation would fill a million pages.
So, if perchance, you catch my glance
Fixed in your direction
'Tis not considered impolite to admire such perfection.

G.McL. & C.McL.

View over the Solway Firth

SHE WASN'T REALLY THAT GOOD-LOOKING

As a fourteen year old at Dumfries Academy I was hit by adolescence and girls . . . and my view of life began to change. This essay demonstrates the mixture of emotions attendant upon biological change.

She wasn't really that good-looking – but I liked her! It's strange. I often like a girl that nobody else really fancied. Some said she was a snob. She was, is . . . but I in my ignorance never really noticed it. I simply went on trying to suppress my only too obvious emotions towards that girl. I tried to act tough, queer, casual. It seldom worked. I knew she had me. She knew too. Recipe for disaster.

That's what made it so bad. If I could have hidden my admiration for her she might not have treated me the way she finally did – a sharp 'I don't want to see you again' that Saturday night. I recall how rotten I felt – gutted. My parents, sister and all my friends, even she, thinks I've fully recovered, forgotten and forgiven. They think I can wipe this mediocre romance of mine from my mind. But I want to keep it green. It is strange, though, I cannot see things quite so vividly as I did then. I'd love to hurt her for hurting me but no doubt in doing so I'd only hurt myself.

Some girls, usually the younger ones, picture me as unfeeling – as a guy who goes out with a girl and drops her – but it's only through fear that I shall become too fond of them and get hurt in the end. I'm a coward, that's obvious, but I can't help it. It's just how I'm made.

When I am at school and see everybody, I feel OK. I see her, then I feel rotten again. I come home, I think about her, and get depressed. My mother thinks I am mad at her. I am, I suppose – very indirectly though. Depression's a terrible thing. I picture it as one person with everyone, everything else, against him. Everybody's nice to his face but they all hate him. I really feel low and have often contemplated suicide but I'm not even brave enough to kill myself.

That's all I really have to say except that a lot of people think I'm a bum, some a queer fellow – I like that. I've always wanted to be thought enigmatic – others don't notice me all that much.

My mother says depression is self-pity. She is probably right. I do feel helluva sorry for myself at the moment.

G.McL.

A SUMMARY OF 'TONIGHT'

*I had only been at Dumfries Academy for about a week when our English teacher, known as
Fat Tam, gave us this 'Ink Exercise'. We were to watch the Cliff Michelmore programme 'Tonight'
and summarise its contents. I was clueless, but my father stepped into the breach and wrote this essay.
Fat Tam was neither fat nor was his name Tam. He was Walter McCall who was to be an inspiration
to me. The essay earned me a reasonable result of 14½/20 but he asked me if
I was German because of the length of Dad's first sentence.*

Cliff Michelmore talked to Mr Smith, the Southern Rhodesian Premier, about the many
problems affecting his country at this time, and although Mr Smith declared himself very
satisfied with his visit here for his talks with the British Prime Minister in connection with the
coming independence of Southern Rhodesia, there still appears to be many difficulties to be
overcome before all parties concerned will be satisfied with the political situation in that part
of Africa. One of the most serious problems is the fact, that, although the coloured population
exceeds the white, less than a tenth of the Parliamentary representatives are coloured people.

There was a commentary on one of the races for the Americas Cup, which took place thirty
years ago, between the British yacht, Endeavour, and the American yacht, Rainbow. It was a
hard fought race between these two splendid craft, but eventually the Endeavour managed to
gain the lead which she held and so won a well deserved victory, but sad to say she was beaten
by the Rainbow in another two races, and so lost the cup. The Americas Cup is a trophy which
British yachtsmen have coveted for many years. Millionaires have lost fortunes in their vain
attempts to bring this prize to Britain. The most notable of those men was Sir Thomas Lipton,
whose ambition was to win this cup no matter what the cost. He built a number of yachts, all of
which he named Shamrock, all to no avail, this will o' the wisp always eluded him.

The Irishman's claim that the shamrock will grow only on Irish ground was placed in doubt
by an English gardener who brought some plants home from Ireland to grow in his greenhouse.

After carefully studying them he claimed that it was just a common weed, several varieties of which grew abundantly in the woods of England. An expert was consulted on the subject and he explained that there are many plants closely resembling the shamrock, but only one was the 'Real McCoy'. This one can be apparently recognised by two distinct grooves on each leaf.

The Shamrock

Kenneth Allsop questioned two men about the various drawbacks which may affect the two big parties in the forthcoming election. The Labour party may find their policy of nationalisation a stumbling block, as this taking over many of the major industries has no doubt the possibility of involving the man in the street with an increase in taxation. On the other hand, Mr Wilson's declared plans for our future Britain had many attractions which so far the Conservative leaders are unable to offer the electorate. One of the greatest drawbacks to the Conservative party may be the inability to produce such a leader. The Premier, by putting the election off until October, may, by his cunning manoeuvre memorably have done as much damage as good to his cause, as there is no doubt that the enlightened man on the street today will prefer a calm intelligent leader to a 'smart Alec'.

MacDonald Hastings, in a Suffolk churchyard at night, gave a very interesting talk on bats and their habits. He was studying the sounds made by bats as they fly. They apparently use these sounds as a sort of radar which enables them to avoid objects flying in the dark.

All these topics added up to a programme which, on the whole, proved quite interesting and educational.

C.McL.

POLITICS

The run-up to the 1964 general election was exciting and the television coverage was gripping.
Sir Alex Douglas-Home often used to shoot on the Buccleuch Estates.

Sir Alec read in the local papers
Of the Labour party and their capers.
He then proceeded up the stairs,
Knelt by his bed to say his prayers.
'Oh Lord, no longer on me frown
Please nail this Harold Wilson down.
I thought you'd landed him a cropper
With the (sad) demise of Gordon Walker
But still he's trying me to down
With the help of Geordie Brown.
Why, just last night, on television
He spoke of me with such derision
My future now is fraught with fears
At the mention of our thirteen years.
Why can't this commoner take heed
That I am of a finer breed.
Why should I try to please the masses?
I'm a member of the Upper Classes!
I promise I'll attend Communion
If you smash the last Trade Union.
Bring these workers to their knees
And save the Tory party please!'

C.McL.

DRUMLANRIG

The Drumlanrig estate of the Duke of Buccleuch stretches from the north of Nithsdale, Durisdeer and Wanlockhead to Closeburn in the south and west to Penport and Keir. The Castle, quadrangular in form, stands on an eminence three miles from Thornhill with commanding views throughout the entire Nith valley.

The estate was granted to the Douglas family by David II of Scotland in 1356. The present family entered into it in 1810.

A picture gallery runs along its northern side for 145 feet and it is here that in 1745 Highlanders of Bonnie Prince Charlie's army spent a night on their retreat from England.

The most popular approach is by Nith bridge off the A76 where there is a beautifully wooded approach almost two miles long. There are gardens and a children's play area. The gardens were once among the finest flower gardens in Scotland of which the 'Paisley shawl' was the best known.

The art collection, open to the public, is amazing and possibly the only place in the world where you could see a Holbein, da Vinci and Rembrandt painting at the same time.

G.McL.

Drumlanrig Castle

THE APOLOGY

The journey to Dumfries Academy involved a daily twenty-eight mile round trip on the bus. The bus stopped en route to pick up other students. There was one very pretty girl from Auldgirth who had rather beautiful legs . . . only one day she caught me looking! I was reported and forced to apologise.

Dear Madam

My apology most certainly must be given
I realise for this wicked act
I'll never get to heaven.
But if from your heart
You could impart
A little bit of sorrow
And when you see me on the bus
Show more of your legs tomorrow!

G.McL.

SUSSIES[1] ON THE BUSES

Doug Gillon is a sports journalist on the The Herald in Glasgow. We have been friends for years.
This is his response to 'The Apology'.

Once ye had atoned for your sins
Did the lassie frae Auldgirth show mair of her pins,
Lasciviously raising her hems?
'Til the only vista that filled up yer eye
Was the wanton expanse of that milken white thigh?
And as she inched those skirts even higher
Did ye feast yer een on yer heart's desire?
Or is she there at Auldgirth still

A staid auld maid, well o'er the hill
A typical biddy as yet unlaid.
Regretting the games she might have played
Still waiting on yon lad McLatchie
Who lusted aye, but dared not catch ye?

Doug Gillon

[1] *Sussies – suspenders*

LOGGING

This was the term used for preparing firewood for winter. It was simple really, in principle. We chopped down trees, sawed them into logs, and burned them. However, they were mature beech and ash. Birch burned best, the others more slowly both retaining and exuding heat.

The trees were felled with an axe, to cut the initial wedge, then completed with a double-handled saw and the whole process took weeks. When, however, the chain-saw or power-saw arrived, the exercise was reduced to no more than a few days.

These pictures show my father, brother, woodsman Bob Cluckie (with saw), and my nephew Carlton (in short trousers), judged later by my father to be an excellent chess player. He also became a second Dan in judo, winning the under 21 British Championships.

My nephew Marvin, Carlton's brother, became a fourth Dan in judo, and was ranked seventh in the world in 1983. He also won a silver medal in the American Open Championships.

G.McL.

From left to right: Carlton, Cy, Neilson, and Bob Cluckie the woodsman

Neilson

Marvin and his friend Marilyn

Bob Cluckie, Cy and Neilson

Cy, Bob and Neilson

ON WINNING

*In 1964-65 I won the Match-play Winter Championship at Dumfries
Academy – not particularly popular for a new boy to the school.*

*Success always seems to be accompanied by criticism, and perhaps awakens the
'Green-eyed yellow monster' in colleagues and school mates.*

You peer down at me, how dare you
I'm worthy of respect –
'Tis I who won, not you at all
That surely you detect.
But still I'm common, that's to you,
You patronise me cruelly.
Let me be base, you know it's true
At golf, I beat you truly!

G.McL.

Greg driving at the seventh hole

THE FLY IN THE INKWELL

Falling in and out of love appears to be an adolescent hazard. These verses are obviously influenced by the American poet, Robert Frost, whom we were studying at the time.

That fly, I think, is wasting time
In trying to escape from all that grime
I'll stay and watch him for a while
Although it's really like a crime.

He surfaces, blue as his eyes his wings with ink,
Begins to climb then slip and sink
I find it quite amusing now
To see him almost reach the brink!

The vain attempts of that poor fly
Resemble, strangely, me – for I
Grasp to keep a memory
Of someone who's not worth a sigh.

But now the ink is o'er my head
I can't remember how she said
'Goodbye'. The memory is gone and lost
The ailing emotions now all dead.

In years to come I'll sit and think
I'll try to reach the inkwell's brink
And be glad to be drowned in all that ink
And be glad to be drowned in all that ink.

G.McL.

TO A CRITIC

You say I'm not so fast as you
When through them I have bored.
You criticise my rugby skill –
How come you've never scored?

G.McL.

KATHLEEN

This poem was written on my sister's eighteenth birthday. She had just won the 'Cock o' the Border' competition with her boyfriend Donald Houston. Donald played guitar and Kate sang. She went on to qualify as a school teacher but taught little as she became a professional singer. Sadly, she died in 1998 at the age of fifty.

Oh lovely is the dawn of day
When the sun shines down the glen.
How sweet to see the fawn at play
Far from the haunts of men.
The blooming heather on the hills,
The music of the mountain stream.
But for beauty rare, nought can compare
With you, my darling, sweet Kathleen.

When Mother Nature smiled on your face
On that cool September morn.
She brought gifts of beauty poise and grace
Her darling to adorn.
To these she added nature sweet
And charming personality.
Then said, when She saw you complete,
'My fondest dream is now indeed reality!'

C.McL.

Kathleen with Donald Houston

KIRKPATRICK McMILLAN

About a mile south of the village of Penpont and a mile and a half south-west of Thornhill is Keir Mill and the former smithy of Courthill. A sandstone tablet on the wall tells us that the first bicycle was built here by the inventor, Kirkpatrick McMillan about the year 1840. Constructed mostly of wood, it had a horse's head on the front as its figurehead. The wheels were of wood shod with iron and a model is preserved in the Dumfries Observatory and Museum (the Camera Obscura). It was driven from the back wheel by cranks fixed on the axle linked to long levers or 'pedals'.

The locals called Kirkpatrick McMillan 'Daft Pate', and he made many other inventions, but none so important as this. There are now over one billion bicycles worldwide.

It is said he rode the machine into Glasgow where he collided with an old lady. A crowd gathered and he was arrested, locked up for causing an obstruction and subsequently fined, although it's said that the magistrate paid his fine in return for a ride on his new machine.

Here was a man of original mind and character who had no financial interest in his invention, which he never patented. He is buried in the Old Churchyard of Keir. His inscription reads, 'The inventor of the bicycle'. He died in 1878.

At the old smithy, the weather-beaten plaque seems understated and uncared for. Despite the interest in his invention, he continued as a blacksmith. Even Queen Victoria had a bicycle.

And so they gazed and still the wonder grew
Daft Pate, 'He builded better than he knew!'

C.McL.

IN THIS SMITHY
THE FIRST BICYCLE
WAS BUILT BY THE
INVENTOR

KIRKPATRICK M^cMILLAN
ABOUT THE YEAR
1840

1939
THE CENTENARY OF
THE BICYCLE
THE NATIONAL COMMITTEE ON CYCLING
HONOURS THE MEMORY OF
KIRKPATRICK MACMILLAN
THE INVENTOR OF THE BICYCLE
He builded better than he knew

Courthill Smithy

53

THERE'S NOTHING THAT I FEEL NOW

Sixteen years old and dumped just before Christmas! The story always old and always new!

There's nothing that I feel now
Only shame; not remorse but
A burning feeling of shame devouring my being.
'Talk not of wasted affection; affection never was wasted'
I only feel that mine was not appreciated.
It was shunned.
I respected her, more so than others.
She was cold and indifferent towards me.
But since her icy character has left me
Spring is coming. I feel better.

G.McL.

THE PRESENT

Then she returned my Christmas present!

I had saved the coppers . . . slowly.
Sentimentally I had saved them
To buy that present.
I had given up my nights with the lads,
Sacrificed my cigarettes . . .
To buy that present.
She sounded different on the phone . . .
Hard, harsh, heartless.
'I've returned your present,
I hope you won't be too offended.'
Hurt, I hung up.
The present came back this morning.
She must have opened it . . .
The Christmas paper had been turned around.
My address on the outside, hers in.
But there was no letter of excuse;
No 'Keep smiling, Greg' – nothing.
That hurts more.
She played with me cruelly.
Crestfallen I gave in.
I am a fool to the world.
More so to her.
Irrevocably to myself!

G.McL.

HOGMANAY

*Four days later I was almost killed when the car
in which I was a passenger crashed and was a write-off.*

Frost – a cold night.
Icy roads, hidden, black.
Roaring engine, exhaust fuming
Speed limit passed – New Year's Eve.
Joking, talking – more speed.
Roaring now, changing gears – more speed
Foot flat down – more speed.
Icy roads.
Front wheels skid – car hits kerb.
Overturns, again, again, again.
- An eternal second.
Rumbling, bumping, crashing – silence
Petrol trickling?
'Everyone OK?'
'Yeah!'
'Let's get out of here'
Car smashed, clothes ruined, drinks forgotten
– New Year's Eve!

G.McL.

Speed limit passed – New Year's Eve

TRAVELS

This was the result of a train journey to London. My companions in the compartment were air crew and were talking of world destinations as though they were on the next corner. I was en route to my brother's house in Folkestone. I don't think this would have impressed them!

When people ask about my travels
There is little I can say to satisfy their curiosity.
For truthfully I have few memories
To reel off in joy, as you can see
I can say, at least I've been to England.
'What part?' they ask
And then my task of interesting them
Makes my poor heart jump.
'I have seen the Folkestone junkies'
I say with pride
'I have been to Piccadilly, seen the hippies'
They're getting satisfied.
'Til gradually they stand and stare.
'Yes I know London, I've been there!'

G.McL.

BRAINS BEAT BUGS

This was supposed to be a tabloid article on the development of penicillin. In those days bacteria, viruses and vaccines were interchangeable. Our journalists are more knowledgeable now!

Yes, it's cheerio to bacteria and fame to Alec Fleming, the brilliant young bacteriologist, once a student under Sir Almroth Wright.

The new anti-bug drug, penicillin, was accidentally discovered by the observant Fleming when he noticed that on a culture plate some moulds growing were inhibited by another. After time-consuming, fatiguing experiments, he eventually made the grade and procured the wonder-vaccine.

But although now a famous member in Medicine's Hall of Fame, this Great Gift to Mankind has returned to his humble laboratory, not content until he has completed his only task in life, the conquest of even greater horizons in bacteriology.

G.McL.

Waterfall on Dalveen Pass

1967

TIM – NO ORDINARY CAT

My mother became annoyed at my father helping me with homework. She would say 'The boy will come to nothing if you keep writing his essays.' However, I'd learned. Mr McCall immediately noticed the change of style and asked if this was all my own work, but he then crossed this comment out and congratulated me on the essay.

Life has never been the same since Tim's dead, broken body was found among the bracken of a roadside wood a mile from my home.

It was my fifth birthday. I went, as usual, up to the farm half a mile from my home to get the milk. When I arrived it seemed that the farmer knew already that it was my birthday. 'Away tae the barn,' he said. 'Choose any one ye want.' I rushed to the barn and there, in a corner on a broken bale of straw, lay a large queen cat with several kittens playing round her. A little black one tried to scuttle away into a hole in the straw but I managed to get it. 'What are ye going tae call him?' asked the farmer after I had thanked him. 'This,' I replied 'is Timmy'.

It was not long before the kitten settled in. He was exceptionally friendly and soon began to pay his way by catching mice and other vermin.

The first signs of winter were appearing. Networks of frosted cobwebs mantled the grey-headed gorse bushes, thick carpets of leaves lay on the ground, and 'Chill November's surly blast began to blow'. The kitten was no longer so. He had grown into a beautiful, glossy-coated cat with white paws and chest and a long, heavy, black tail which, when he was on the prowl, trailed low behind him giving him a panther-like appearance. He followed me nearly everywhere. He accompanied me half way to school every morning and then went hunting until I returned at night, pouncing out at the spot where we had parted.

At last Spring arrived. Bright flowers appeared and the fields began to shine in a covering of succulent green grass, the sight of which whets the palate of flocks of sheep after a long winter. It was the beginning of the pheasant-rearing. My father, as usual, had several crops of newly-hatched chicks on the field, and was guarding them, with the utmost care, against vermin and other pests. Timmy, too, seemed to understand the gravity of

60

the situation and often he brought, to the door, a stoat or weasel which had been prowling about the coops. He seemed to have cast aside some of his feline instincts because he never interfered with the pheasants, although he killed many other species of wild birds.

Every year, he guarded the pheasants, crouching low down among the long grass of the field, watching, waiting, and pouncing upon any unsuspecting animal which chanced to pass his way, cruelly lengthening the process of its execution by allowing it to escape and then catching it again until eventually it was too terrified to move, when the final stroke was delivered and the creature lay, its body broken and gashed, at his feet.

The 'Glorious Twelfth' was approaching and I obtained a job as a grouse-beater. When I returned, Tim, as was his habit, was waiting for me and pounced out upon me, grabbing my leggings with his long claws and making every effort to tear them in the process.

One evening when I returned, no Tim appeared. This continued for several days and each evening, although I was tired, I set out for all the neighbouring farms to make enquiries about him. Eventually a lady from the nearby village of Cample heard this and visited us. 'The lads of the village say they found a big black cat lying on the road, run-over by a car, and threw it over the dyke into the wood' she said. I thanked her, but even as I did so my eyes grew red and heavy and I was unable to prevent the tears which followed in great abundance, almost blinding me.

It was Timmy whose broken body lay among the brown, blood-stained bracken. His tongue hung limply from the side of his mouth and one of his lacerated shoulder-blades protruded through his glossy, black fur, clotted with blood.

He was buried the following day in the shade of a holly bush. It was with a feeling of deep despondency that I laid him in his last resting-place and placed a little white cross above his grave. Even to this day I still at times stand gazing at the little cross and remember the happy times we had together.

18½ / 20 ~~Is this all your own?~~ Excellent. Your device of foreshadowing the sad conclusion is quite splendid. Well done!

G.McL.

1967

THE FOX HUNT

The first and last fox hunt I was ever on was just before my eighth birthday.

The living-room clock was striking seven as my father and I left the house and set off down the road, our dog, Gyp, following close behind us.

This was my first fox hunt. I was now seven years old and skipped and ran trying to keep up with my father who strode out in front of me with his gun under his arm.

The overcast sky began to break and the silver frost on the ground sparkled brightly in the rays of sunlight peeping through the clouds. After walking some distance we surprised a hare amongst some rushes. It immediately bounded away but my father didn't attempt to shoot it. No disturbance was wanted until the forward guns were into position in preparation for driving the wood.

In the distance we saw a group of men telling jokes, smoking, and laughing. Fierce little terriers snapped and growled at one another. Gyp cocked his ears and strutted towards them, stiffly erecting the hair on the nape of his neck. The other dogs ran towards him, baring their teeth, but were soon stopped, 'Get out o' that' roared the head-keeper, and the dogs, cringeing, went to their masters' heels.

'Tie your hankie tae a stick and follow me,' said one keeper. He told me to stay in a field and wave my flag if I saw a fox. I lay down and listened to the men shouting and whistling as they were driving one of the nearby woods. All of a sudden the shout 'Tally ho!' was raised. There was a confusion of shouts, yelps and shots. Then followed a volley of free-language. The fox had been missed.

The men dragged themselves dejectedly from the wood muttering under their breath. The wily creature had managed to escape once and now the chances of killing it were very dim. This they all knew and, with their dogs trailing behind them, they moved over some fields to another wood.

Again the men lined out. This time I was allowed to go with my father and aided greatly by yelling at the top of my voice.

A burn traced its way through the wood, meandering round tree-roots and rocks. Frightened wood-pigeons fluttered out of the trees, covering me with a shower of prickly pine-needles. Suddenly, from a clump of dead bracken, broke away a brown animal. For a few moments I stood in amazement, then I realised that I had put a fox to flight. With a broken voice I cried 'Tally ho!' and ran to my father, thoroughly terrified. I managed to reach the side of the wood just in time to see the fox cross a field. It suddenly stumbled, and then as it fell and rolled over came the report of a gun.

I wandered over to the body of the little brown animal stretched out limply beside the burn. The fur on its long, bushy tail, tipped with black, blew in the breeze. I was slightly disappointed. This creature looked too peaceful to be a marauder, yet when the terriers caught its scent they rushed upon it, tearing it apart.

The stench of the fox was overpowering. The dogs, covered in blood, drank from the burn and chased each other over the field. The keepers smoked and talked, thoroughly satisfied with their day. I thought that it was all very cruel and, with tears of pity in my eyes, I crossed the fields and made for home.

G.McL.

MORTON CASTLE

The ruins of this former Douglas stronghold stand on a steep green bank above a narrow loch. Nearby, in the days of Wallace, the main road (then a ridge) extended through Nithsdale to England. Wallace, after pursuing the English down the ridge, defeated them in 1297 near Dalswinton.

Morton Castle is defended on all sides, except the south-west, by a loch which was formed by a dam. A deep ditch, or fossa, no doubt caused by a drawbridge, would protect it. It is to the east of Thornhill, and after ascending the Burn Brae and pausing for breath, you'll see in the south the bold outline of Criffel on Solway. The road to the left leads to Morton.

There is an old legend that Lady Morton falls in love with Edward, a young servant at the Castle, but he is already in love with Agnes who lives with her parents by Carron Water. Lady Morton informs her husband that Edward has shown interest in her and in a tremendous storm the Earl of Morton incarcerates him in the dungeon to die of starvation. The Lady, however, feeds him and she suggests Agnes pleads for his life and freedom. However, the Earl, more angry than ever, demands two unbroken colts to be brought:

> 'Gae fetch me yon twa wild steeds
> Which gang on Knockenshaw
> And 'fore I either eat or drink
> Tae death I will him draw.'

Poor Edward is bound hand and foot and tied to the animals' tails. They set off in different directions:

> Away, away, the rapid pair
> Still flew on wings of fear
> Along the wild and rugged road
> That leads to Durisdeer.

Edward's head fell off at the 'Head' near Durisdeer, where an upright stone marks the spot. Lads, watch out for married Scottish women!

The ruins today are still impressive and would make an excellent backdrop for a film. (Morton Castle was later used in the film 'The Thirty-nine Steps' starring Robert Powell)

G.McL.

Churchyard at Durisdeer

MY FUTURE HAS BEEN CHANGED

I passed my Highers in 1967 and decided to study Medicine.
I also decided to do a sixth year. I continued with Sciences but also studied French and English.
It would be five years before I wrote another essay in English, although
my love of poetry continued.

My future has been changed
And all because of that little scrap of paper!
My life and outlook rearranged
And all because of that little scrap of paper!
The print is cold.
My thoughts are sold
To gain these passes.

Others have the same paper
But the name and print are different too
Although the paper looks the same
They who are happy, indeed are few!

Two roads there forked for me to choose.
Two roads in Life? – What nonsense!
I chose the one that looked the best.
And that's made all the difference

G.McL.

Looking towards Nith Linns

Woodland walk near Drumlanrig Castle

IN LOVE AGAIN

This time it was to last for three years!

You cannot picture her
Although she is human
You cannot annoy her
Although a woman
Is easily annoyed.
My time's enjoyed, employed
In thinking
In drinking
In smoking
In dreaming
In seeming to forget
But yet I can't.

G.McL.

A NAME IS NOT BEAUTIFUL

A name is not beautiful
But it's what it connotes that promotes the joy.
It rings in my ears
No other girl has the same
And tears run down the face of this boy
Whenever he hears that name.

G.McL.

Mennock Water

Woodland pool at Drumlanrig

March 1968

IT SEEMS STRANGE

I sit
It seems strange that I
Should exchange a sigh
And glances with you.

I knit
Together our souls and try
To prove beyond doubt, though shy
My reasons not untrue

I flit
From thought to thought and nigh
I come to say, 'Goodbye'
For fear of Love chills me through.

I am at last resigned
In Love I find a contentedness,
A confidence –
A soul repairer
No longer am I blind.

G.McL.

THE MOON LAUGHED AT US

Was she pregnant? We were both still at school. Our careers flashed in front of our eyes.

The moon laughed at us in our joy
We lived our lives in love
And nothing could move the feelings that we had.
But very soon we found that
Who mistrusts Fate
Lies very, very flat.
Of late, we've been afraid
A mistake has been made
And Life is not now gold and lace.
Fate, seemingly the kind,
Seemingly healer to the mind
Seemingly making us unblind . . .
Has kicked us in the face!

. . . She wasn't!

G.McL.

A walk above Durisdeer

ABSENCE NOT FONDER RENDERS

I was Sir Toby Belch in the Academy production of Twelfth Night. One of the courtesans (sic) took a fancy to me – and I to her.

How I am weak, I must not yield
'Tis but an idle fancy here.
She's not comparable to you, my dear
Her selfish motives are made clear
Your love shall be my shield.
I look on her and feel an urge but yet
I am, by oath, forbidden to take her in my arms
I am, by oath, forbidden to experience the charms
And wonders I could get.
Absence not fonder renders . . .
It makes the heart forget!

G.McL.

Looking towards Thornhill from the school playing fields

HOW WILL IT BE?

The prospect of going to University both excited and terrified me.
My girlfriend, who was two years younger than me, planned to go to
Glasgow University and did – only we'd split up by then.
The poem is prophetic.

I love you now but how will it be in six years?
Will there be tears . . .
And 'in between' romances?
Or will our love be such that ends
And leaves us weak and lost for life?
My thoughts are fixed
But yours are mixed – you're young
Have fun and joy with others 'til you settle.
But I would rather we remained together
And time stood still.

G.McL.

The River Nith near Drumlanrig

MY SONS

*This verse was written by my father just before I
left Blacknest to go to Glasgow University. My brother Neilson,
who was fourteen years older than me, had left home in 1953 and my sister
Kate left in 1966. I suppose that Dad was reflecting on the times we
had spent together – rabbit-trapping, pheasant-rearing, fox-hunting
and bird-nesting, as we called it – an emotional
look at the past.*

I've wandered many a weary mile
Along Life's lonely road
I've witnessed scenes of beauty
Which lightened up my load.
But no greater joy my heart could fill
As long as my life runs
Than that which overwhelms me
When I'm thinking of my sons!

C.McL.

The Lad, sawing

Neilson, the Boxer

THE HOUSE ON THE MOOR

*This poem was by way of thanks for a favour done by the owner of Ardcriffel, the
house on the moor. These favours were usually 'tit for tat' and rarely involved the exchange of money.
Perhaps, in return for having a fox killed by Dad, the occupier gave him potatoes or vegetables from
his fields – a common practice in Dumfries and Galloway at that time.*

By land that's kissed by Solway's tide
Close by dark Lochar spreading wide,
Ardcriffel stands, its walls secure,
A stalwart guardian of the Moor.
Could mortal mind turn o'er the pages
And read what's happened through the ages?
What deeds of valour here 'twould trace?
What scenes of joy or grief took place
Within your stout stone walls?
How many simple party dances?
How many true and false romances?
Alas, your walls of stone and lime
Have kept no record for my rhyme,
So I perforce, must drift in dreams
Through your varying by-gone scenes
And pray the present occupier
Finds love and joy by your warm peat fire.

C.McL.

Sunrise over Solway's tide

THE GAMEKEEPER

My father was in his sixty-third year when he wrote this. I think the toughness of his existence was catching up with him. This was his last poem. I went to University that year. 'You're on your own now son,' he said. I felt I was going to war – not higher education!

The autumn morning slowly dawns.
The keeper rises, stretches, yawns
Then with the morn's ablutions past
Partakes his ham and eggs breakfast.
With a fond farewell to his family's faces
He goes to one of the meeting places
Where all are bundled in a truck
Just like a farmer loading muck.
Inside there is no room to quarrel
They're packed like herring in a barrel
Eleven dogs and seventeen men
Crushed in a space six feet by ten!

When they arrive at Wanlockhead
Some are sick, but none are dead.
The journey was no bed of roses
Their superiors view them down their noses.
The working class are overrated
Their value overestimated.
Why get annoyed if one should smother
A press advert will get another!

Though some complain that they feel ill
They'll struggle up the steepest hill
To drive the grouse out o'er the butts
Just for the pleasure of these nuts.
All day there's nought but grouse (and grousing!)
Then home it is – to start delousing.
Some may go out on the spree
But still hunt for that damned grouse flea
Or when they sit to watch the telly
They'll find one crawling on their belly,
And they're addressed as of ill fame
Does a keeper have a Christian name?

There's no doubt that the keeper's lot
Isn't really very hot.
Throughout the drive there's lots of bawling
If his dog runs in, the guns start squalling.
But add to this – there's nothing cheaper
Than the service of a keeper.
His life he'd surely find exciting
And his reward be more inviting
If he left these lonely hills and glens
To scratch the midden with the hens.
His treatment would be less uncivil
Gathering firewood for the devil.
If it's for punishment you pray,
Be a keeper. You will have your way!

C.McL.

View from the hills above Durisdeer

Cyril McLatchie, Gregor McLatchie and Jean McLatchie

. . . then in 1974 I graduated from Glasgow University